HOW TO SCOORE HIGH GRADES IN SCHOOL

JOHN OTOYO

ISBN: 9798848951875

TABLE OF CONTENT

INTRODUCTION

Physical examination is a way of testing the ability of the students by the teacher to observe if the student has acquired the relevant knowledge and skills required in that very subject. The purpose of examination is not to kill students as most of the students supposed it to be that is what makes them afraid each time they are faced with exams.

A student is expected to perform excellently well after being taught in class by the teacher or lecturer during the term or semester before the commencement of exams, so the idea of grading students in school is to show how well the student has understood the subject that was taught in class, and adequately express them into writing to convince the teacher that he or she has truly understood what was taught during the term. Exams grading also help to compare the ability of students in the same class or school to identify those that respond perfectly to the lessons and assess those that require improvement and attention.

It has been discovered from findings that not more than 40% of the entire students in a class pass their exams with undisputable high grades and distinction, majority score below average and others wallow in failure. This has been a major problem that attacks the educational sector since its inception in our society.

Some students might start well from Nursery to primary school level, but when they get to high school and college level they begin to depreciate in their grades. Other students can't just explain why they are not getting good grades, even when they try all their best, study their books, and do their homework and assignments, but they still find themselves struggling to pass their exams. Many factors have been considered to affect the efficiency of a student's performance in school some of which has been carefully discussed in this book. While the issues of failing grades in school is critical and require urgent intervention, this book contains timely and vital information to help every student discover the hidden potentials in them and extract them to accomplish their academic dreams. HOW TO SCORE HIGH GRADES IN SCHOOL IN SCHOOL is a hand held book designed to help the students at all levels of Education, go through the school with courage and vitality that will help them attain a desirable success in their academic results. But it is good for us to note that success in academics is possible and not very far from us; can we leverage the potential within us to overcome academic challenges that we face every day? Yes we can, we can become whatever we dream or hope to become in future so make up your mind today to become the best you can ever imagine.

HAPPY READING

CHAPTER ONE

WHY GO TO SCHOOL?

The question **why go to school** is a very important question every student in school environment needs to ask him/her as well as provide answers likewise. It is to help them distinguish themselves from their peers and friends who choose not to go to school at all. It will also help every students possess a strong reason and a burning desire to see their dreams accomplished in their academic pursuit. If you are a student reading this book, you need to personally ask yourself the above question and try to provide a convincing answer to proof that you are really aware and fully understand the purpose for going to school and if you cannot provide an answer to the above question right now, don't worry just keep on reading because you will soon find out what your own purpose for going to school is.

A student without a clear understanding of the purpose of going to school is like a vehicle on the road without an intended destination. Your purpose for Education is your personal aim, target or your goal concerning your future career. Before you took the decision of going to school as an individual, or before your parents and guardian made plans of sending you to school, there was a purpose or a strong reason why you need the education and this purpose must be clearly defined to give you a specified direction in your career. You don't need to make it a secret you must be aware of it and properly stated out clearly. It is this purpose that is well-defined will constantly remind you of your life ambition and position you for success. Your purpose also becomes an inner drive that gives you the energy and motivation to consistently work hard and remain focused in your studies until you achieve your goal.

Remember when purpose is not defined, abuse is inevitable. Your purpose is what will attach value to your to your education and help you pay maximum attention to your studies at all-times despite the challenges that might come your way. Your purpose also gives you an insight to your end as you begin to see yourself becoming that which you proposed to become in future from your present. It is your purpose that will determine how you end whether it will be pleasant or horrible. The graduation day is always a day of great expectation where everyone connected to you will like to see you graduate with flying colors, but it is often quite unfortunate to note that many students who started well at the beginning of their studies may not be able to graduate on the final day of graduation because there was no purpose in their heart towards their education. This is why many students fail and keep on failing without seeking for early solution to remedy them from the misfortune of failure.

However, as we continue to discuss on this subject matter about the purpose behind your education, we will discover many purposes or reasons that countless students propose in their hearts as they go to school and we shall quickly take a look at them briefly.

SOME EXAMPLES OF PURPOSES/REASONS IDENTIFIED ARE

1. To Satisfy My Parents/Guardians Wishes

Some students only go to school as a result of the obligation by which they feel they have to fulfill the wish of their Parent/Guardians, Relatives, and Government. Though these groups of people may have good intention for the education of their wards but the goal is often forfeited because these set of students who have the orientation of fulfilling their parent's wishes often do not align their ambition with that of their Parents/Guardians and as such do not take their education serious. Students in this category only attend school because they are compelled by their parents to go to school. They put on their uniforms, leave the home, then go to school only to play around in the class, become obstinate to teachers instruction, and even go as far as roaming around the streets because their concept is not aligned to that their Parents/Guardians purpose and most time the Parents/Guardian do not communicate the reason for their Education properly to the level of their understanding. It is proven beyond every reasonable doubt that students in this category always end up with failing grades this is because they are constantly struggling with an idea that is against their wish and was not originally initiated by them. Sometimes their Parents/Guardian design their career to study a course that they do not really like but since they do not have any choice of their own to resist they accept it, go to school and keep struggling all through they always have at the back of their minds that whatever they are studying in school belongs to their parents and so their purpose here is to fulfill their parent's desires.

2. **To Be Like Others**

Students in this category go to school because they want to also be like their peers and measure up with them either because they look flamboyant, flashy, responsible, or maybe to spread information around town among friends and colleagues that they are also going to school. Case study of these group of students are those in tertiary institutions who only concentrate on imitating and copying others in the way they dress, walk, or act and channel all their thoughts and energy towards emulating what others do at the expense of their education. They are easily carried away by other people appearance and looks, and they hastily learn bad habits. This takes their focus away from their education and most times they end up not fulfilling their dream.

3. **To Build A Career**

Students in this group are those who go to school with a personal ambition and the purpose of building a professional career for themselves which they have targeted for a long time either because they admire that career or maybe they have been destined to function that area; and as they get to school, they work very hard to get themselves equipped for this purpose so that they will become relevant in their career and to provide solution for their country, community, and family. This singular purpose alone can constantly infuse energy in them throughout their stay in school. They will do all they can to put in more effort, become more serious and committed to their studies. Their purpose here fertilizes their passion to pursue a profitable career which they have chosen by themselves to make a difference and they know that they can only arrive there through their present education. Note here they do all they can to achieve their personal dream because it concerns their future.

4. **To Own Certificate**

Some students are also found in school only because of the certificate they will get at the end of their studies. They are not concerned about any other thing; all they are particular about is to acquire the certificate. They may either need it just to proof to somebody that they went to school, or maybe to upgrade their level and status in the offices they work, or for job promotion pursuit or to back up their trade for those in business etc. The focus of these set of students lies on the certificate, because that is their primary target. Sometimes they wish the years of studies in school should be reduced or fast forwarded so that they could obtain their certificate as fast as possible and leave the school environment. For these ones their primary purpose is just to get the certificate alone.

5. **To Fit into The Society**

These sets of students are found in school because they want to be celebrated and highly respected in the society and association which they belong or find themselves in; since they do not want to be mocked by friends and relatives or looked down upon the resolve to go school. An illiterate man in a changing world will usually feel inferior and unwanted by colleagues and friends, so to change that notion, some of them pick up the challenge of going to school just to be noticed in the society and prove a point that they are not illiterate. Their purpose here is to be noticed in the society.

6. **To Get A Good Job**

These categories of students are found in school for the purpose of getting a good job after their graduation. So they work hard to acquire the necessary skills and trainings that will qualify them for any job they may apply for. Their purpose here is to have a good paid job with their qualification at end of their studies.

7. **To Upgrade Educational Status**

Some students are also found in the schools for the purpose of upgrading their academic status either by learning, research, investigation, etc. so they go to school in order to upgrade their academic and intellectual reservoir. These group of students are more focused with their academic pursuit they are just ready to explore any information to expand their educational scope.

All these examples mentioned above and many more are diverse purposes that exist among students within the school environment. Whichever area of these categories listed above, is your primary aim of going to school, you must clearly state it out in black and white as this will ignite your passion for excellence and place a permanent picture in front of you concerning your future.

If you are going to school for the purpose of building a career for instance, you need to correctly specify the actual area of discipline you are building your career upon, and then discover the various principles and challenges that is accompanied with the choice of your career, then if you begin to work hard towards it tirelessly, you will eventually see yourself operate fully in that facet of your chosen career and at the end of your studies, you will have every reason to be happy with yourself because your purpose was correctly laid out for the foundation of that Success. You will also notice that you will begin to find education more interesting and the readiness for studies any time you are called upon will naturally awaken within you. This new practice will automatically ease the work of your teacher and lecturers because the enthusiasm they need to see and love for education is already kindled within you to study and even go the extra mile to research what was taught in class the previous day on your own in order to obtain a more excellent result and satisfy your inner desire for your genuine quest.

This takes us to what I call PASSION an inward energy. It reduces the effect of failure and increases the determination to succeed. Purpose produces passion and success responds to passion. No passionate person has ever become a complete failure before, because what other students see as a difficult subject, a passionate student will consider it easily achievable. When you are passionate about your career you will naturally resist failure and the willingness to discipline yourself and follow systematically all the procedures and fundamental principles to make you a complete success will automatically be activated within you.

But when the exact purpose of your going to school is not properly defined, passion will be lost and the opportunity of going to school will be abused. Education is meant to be an investment and the student must deliberately subscribe to all the disciplines to produce a positive and enviable result. The teachers will only be fulfilled when they the students perform very well in tests and exams because it is proof that what they taught you was not a wasted resource. Your first journey to high grades begins with the identification of your purpose for going to school this is the underground magic behind the story of every successful student.

So clearly define your purpose for going to school and seriously examine it carefully this will help you to be in constant tune with your passion and bring out the best in you as a student. If you still become purposeless up till now, after reading this book please consult your school counselor or academic advisor and get more help to develop a personal a purpose for your education and stick to it because this is what will qualify you for high grades and success in your academic pursuit.

CHAPTER TWO

10 REASONS WHY STUDENTS FAIL IN EXAMS

There are a lot of reasons why students completely fail in exams or sometimes regularly score below average level due to a number of factors, but we shall look at only 10 points of these reasons in this chapter. I will also like to mention here that every student in one way or the other, have experienced failure before no matter how intelligent they might claim to be. So if you are a victim of any of these circumstances mentioned below, do not be afraid because they are just an eye opener to give you update information of the different symptoms of failure and what leads to backwardness in academic pursuit so that as you see these signs anytime you will be positioned to readily avoid them.

Let's quickly have a look at the various reasons why students fail in school.

1. DISTRACTION

Distraction leads to destruction; and it comes in form of amusing pleasure and self-gratification. Sometimes when you are carried away by distraction you will begin to enjoy its activities and anyone who tries to caution you at that time will become your enemy because you think he might be disturbing you or disrupting you from enjoying yourself at that time. The activities involved in distraction is so enticing that while other students are receiving lessons in the class room, some are so distracted and extremely carried away to go behind walls to feel high with smoking, drinking, playing, and all other form of vices which will gradually damage their brains and knock out their mental capacities.

Other forms of distraction include idling away with aimless chat, online chat rooms with social networks, illicit sex, partying, and playing unintelligent games all at the detriment of their studies. All these activities are often enticing and sweet to enjoy but they lead to endless regrets and failure. You need to avoid these activities and engage yourself wisely with healthy extra curriculum activities that will profit your academic pursuit because these forms of distraction can swerve you away from your focus and damage your academic career.

2. EXCUSES

Excuses are bedrock to failure, when you know what to do and refuse to do it due to laxity and irresponsibility on your part you resort to excuses to exempt yourself from the consequences. Some students are professional excuse givers, they give excuses over every little thing and challenges they encounter even when they have what it take to overcome them.

Most times the excuses they give are planned lies and irrelevant. They have excuses to give why they did not submit their assignment on time, another for why they did not read and study in the night, another for why they did not attend classes the previous day, and another for why they even fail the test. They cannot conquer the same situation other student's conquered. Even when they see some other students soaked with rain to go for lessons they remain at home to warm themselves with hot water and cover their blankets because they will always have something to say as an excuse for every situation. Excuses give birth to failure; whenever you cover up anything you have the ability to conquer with flimsy excuses that means you have failed in responding to your ability because without the same excuses you can still do something positive and succeed like others. Avoid excuses and take responsibility of your action if you want to succeed.

3. BAD BEHAVIOUR IN CLASS

The strength of your moral behavior will contribute enormously to your success in school and exams, most actions and habits demonstrated by some students in class today is traceable to the weakness of their moral willpower which can lead to serious distraction and failure.

Some of these bad behaviors are sleeping while lesson is going on, excessive noisemaking, chewing gum every second, making indecent phone calls while receiving lecture, applying makeup in classroom, and practicing other similar bad habits during school hours. It is expected that students should conduct themselves in a substantial disciplinary manner and observe good etiquette while in the classroom receiving lectures so as to concentrate fully on the teacher and receive the lessons with utmost satisfaction.

Every student should be encouraged to behave well and pay close attention to the teachers while putting away bad behaviors such as mentioned above and then take advantage of the lessons to perform well in exams.

4. PROCRASTINATION

When you habitually put off your assignments and studies for the future, then you are heading to failure. Procrastination is the mother of laziness and whatever you postpone to do tomorrow will always remain there for you to come back and complete it so i think your Education should be highly prioritized in the scheme of your priorities. The habit of procrastination has become a daily lifestyle and routine of many students. They just approach their academic work very lightly and frivolously whereas this result to laxity and misplaced priority, they don't do their assignments and homework on time, they don't read as at when due, neither do they develop a study guide for themselves because they habitually suspend their study for another day at the detriment of their Education.

Even when an opportunity of perusing relevant information that will be of great benefit to their studies present itself to them freely, they feel reluctant about it and kick it off. But when the need arises to make use of that information they had free access to the other day, they become automatically confused because they have missed it. Procrastination is dangerous and risky; it will stop you from getting what you desire even when you work so had at the closing hour to catch up with the workload. Always remember to do what you are supposed to do firstly on time before you consider any other option.

5. MISSING CLASSES

There is so much harm that missing classes can cause to a student's education. However, many students do not have prior knowledge about this monster this is why they continually fall into this trap as it consistently keeps them at the seat of failure. Most students consider it normal to avoid classes due to one reason or the other that best suites them; they miss their lessons, miss their tests and practical class, and even go as far as missing their exams. Maybe this action might be because they hate the teacher handling a particular subject in that school, or perhaps they don't like the subject itself, or they don't just want to be in that class.

Missing classes is very dangerous and can cause a lot of harm to your Education because there are some topics that are discussed in classroom which may not be found in your notes and textbooks. Also some students who frequently attend classes may not need to read too much of the textbooks and notes to pass their exams, they will easily recall what was taught in class once they are challenged with any question on the subject they learned.

6. LACK OF PREPARATION

Lack of preparation for exams can diminish the confidence of a student and make him or her feel impromptu each time he is requested to take test or exams on any subject. Preparation for the task ahead equips you with the necessary gadget to perform impressively when the need arise but most student lack the ability to prepare for their exams in advance and this leads to recurrent failure. They only remember their books when they notice that the timetable for exams is out and if they did not prepare beforehand, they develop exams sickness.

Some students also try to hasten up their reading process, as they gather past questions and notebooks whenever exam time is fast approaching but all these efforts prove abortive due to inadequate preparation. This kind of approach towards your Education can never lead to academic success. Each student should be willing to prepare for exams ahead of time without compulsion to obtain excellent grades.

7. READING OFF PEAK PERIOD

Every student has an off peak and a peak period for reading. Your peak period is when you assimilate more and understand anything you read as fast as possible without any infringement. These are seasons and times when you enjoy the smooth flow of your personal studies and research.

Your off-peak period is when you find it difficult to understand what you are reading at particular time. These are times when your mind is crowded with so many things and disturbed with challenges for a desire not yet met or maybe your thought not in complete tune with the flow of your studying schedule. Most students who continuously fail in exams have been affirmed that they do their reading during off peak periods and this is not a healthy way for studying.

To appreciate your peak period, you need to discover the best time that is suitable for you to read and comprehend easily. Some people like reading in the night hours or afternoon, some may like reading early hours of the morning, others love reading only at night but cannot read at noon time or morning hours. There are also some people who enjoy reading with music and noise while others may not even try it. Some students also enjoy reading while they are hungry but others may not want to try reading while hungry so whatever is the case with you discover your own peak period and make good use of it. If you keep on reading during your off-peak period, you will not comprehend your lessons as much as you could.

8. HATRED FOR SUBJECTS

Many students hold grievous hatred for some subjects without tangible reasons. They just conclude that the subject is too difficult and complicated. These groups of students pay more attention and practice to the subjects which they perform better and enjoy most. Sometimes they decide to hate those subjects because they don't like the teacher that handles it or because their friends and classmate is not offering that subject but generally these subjects are sometimes compulsory for them to study and pass to have comprehensive information that will be valuable to their career. Rather they choose to hate these subjects without cause.

Remember you can't have whatever you hate. You don't need to hate any subject or teacher that teaches you in school because if you fail you will not have anybody to blame neither the teacher nor the subject you hated.

9. **TOO MUCH PRESSURE**

Parents often put pressure on their children to get good grades and if they do not accomplish their desire to the level of their expectation, they punish them severely and this can paralyze the student's ability to make progress and make them fail again the next time. Sometimes this action by Parents/Guardians makes certain students feel they are not good enough to be appreciated and encouraged so their self-esteem remains dim and diminish every day.

Students need to be appreciated and encouraged by their Parents/Guardians for their little effort to boost their self-confidence for a better performance. Talking them down and mentioning those their past failures whenever they go wrong will make them loose their self-esteem in school.

Also, some parents over work their wards with much labor like washing of plates, selling at the shops, hawking around the streets, etc. by the time the children are set for studies, they become so tired and sleepy to assimilate lessons.

10. POVERTY

Poverty is another reason why some students fail in school. This is most prevalent in the areas where free education system is not practiced whereas the students need to source for their own school fees and levies. Even in the areas where the free education is provided by the government in terms of school fees waivers, text books, exercise books, etc. the problem of poverty still persist with a strong presence and influence on the students performance due to poor economic condition of their family to provide basic amenities of life.

Education is tasking and demanding. One who needs to go to school has to be properly funded and sponsored before he or she can venture into this project. Poverty has caused many students to completely drop out from school. A student who is in school needs some money to take care of his personal needs, health needs, material needs, shelter, etc. If these basic provisions are not in place, the student may find it difficult to survive the challenges of passing exams and catering for themselves at the same time.

The effect of poverty can also expose the academic life of the student to suffer embarrassment and shame which can easily swing their focus away.

CHAPTER THREE

TAPPING INTO THE POWER OF STUDYING FOR SUCCESS

Studying is the most frequent word commonly used to address every student in high school and colleges to inspire them and help them concentrate with their education to perform well in their exams. So, the word STUDY is not a new word in the vocabulary of every student and in the context of academic pursuit.

However it is necessary to note that at every phase of life and career, this unique quality called STUDY is required to foster excellent performance in education, career, business, vocation, in all facet of life. So the power of studying cannot be ignored because when you study effectively, it generates boldness in you to confidently talk about any subject you major in.

Studying is an opportunity to gather relevant information and make reference to the vast resources available in various forms such as in books, eBooks, articles, journals and other related materials that are applicable to your field of study; and then while studying extract vital information suitable for your use. As you keep on to study diligently you will definitely become conversant with any topic that your teacher has discussed with you the previous day in class and this will always remain fresh in your memory ready for any moment you may need it.

Furthermore, your study life will give you a wider reach to your research, and the level of your understanding will begin to improve rapidly with a high volume of knowledge which will gradually expand. This practice will enable you pass any exams that will be presented to you at any time in your field of study.

If you observe carefully, you will notice that many students, who obtain extremely bad grades in school, are those students who do not place serious attention on the power of studying and this is the reason why they keep on struggling in order to pass their exams, test, assignments, and homework. Sometimes studying can be very boring and repetitive but you can't really pass any exams without taking proper cognizance of the power of studying. This is the only habit that will assist you to perform well without looking out for any form of cheating and myopic shortcuts.

Let me also make mention here that so much emphasis is always placed on the word studying for students by Parents/Guardian, teachers, counselors, and relations but it is quite unfortunate to notice that these students are told to study hard with the usual language of STUDY but they are not being told about the steps and actions they need to take and how they will do the studying on their own profitable. Studying require certain procedures and strategies that must be followed by anyone who desires to produce an excellent result. Listed below are five practical steps you need to utilize to help you develop a well-organized strategy to study effectively and perform better in exams.

STEPS TO EFFECTIVE STUDY

STEP 1.

- PAY ATTENTION IN CLASS

Try to develop good listening ears and pay close attention to tutors when receiving lessons. put extra effort to do more of listening than talking, listening extensively to your teacher in this manner will give you maximum concentration on the lecture; and help you appreciate everything the teacher is saying with no bridge of gap to grab almost all the points that was discussed. In communication, for correct information to be properly passed on, one of the both parties must be the listener while the other is the communicator. Listening with concentration and observation will give you full capacity for easy comprehension. If you make it as a routine to constantly pay attention in class, you will be well positioned to always ask intelligent questions and your teacher will be excited to explain those things you did not understand too well to your satisfaction. Is this is not a beautiful way to learn? Secondly, you will notice that in answering exam questions or test, you will quickly recollect those things you were taught in class simply because you listened very attentively.

STEP 2.

- TAKE GOOD NOTES

The notes you take in class everyday are very important and they serve as your number one reference point. Most of what you will find on test and exams come from the discussions you had in the classroom and the notes you took down during the learning session. If your teacher draws a diagram on the board copy it down on your note book it will be a good resource for your revision and personal study.

Don't wait until the teacher is gone before you start asking for notes to copy from your classmates. Endeavour to be present in class and take intensive notes on everything that is discussed in class. If possible have a different notebook for rewording it after lessons then review it every night before going to bed; and when the exams come remembering what you learned and studied will be a snap.

STEP 3.

- MAKE STUDY GUIDE FOR YOURSELF

It is ideal to study every day before and after exams but to be an exceptional student, you must get yourself organized by developing and mapping out a timetable for your private study. This time table will have to cover your daily activities like, games, lunch, pleasure time, study and break period. This is more effective and helpful during holidays and free periods.

Your timetable will help you accommodate your daily responsibilities without hurting your academic pursuit. It is important for you to also balance your social activities, study habits, and spiritual lifestyle for effective development so that none will suffer. Allocating time for every activity will help you implement your plans on a daily basis.

STEP 4.

- SET GOALS FOR YOURSELF

Goals are road map to your destination and they must be very realistic and achievable. You must have a target point in your mind on what kind of grade you want to get out of school and clearly define them by writing them out on a board sheet or card and then paste it in front of your door post or study table.

As you set these goals make sure you attempt to reach them and improve on them on daily basis. You should climb from the lower level to the higher level systematically e.g. from C to B and then A and finally A+ depending on your academic vibrancy, aiming at an A+ right away could amount to over ambition and make your goals seem unreached.

Let your goals grow progressively and then you will feel fulfilled at the end.

STEP 5.

- GET CLOSER TO YOUR TEACHER

Teachers and lecturers are open to answer any question asked by their student as long as it is in connection with the course of study he or she lectures in school. Don't be afraid of them they will not bite or harm you in fact they know what is on test and exams so they can help you understand anything that is disturbing you academically only if you can humble and conduct yourself in a good manner to approach them with boldness and self-esteem.

Teachers are good resources for students and they cannot be ignored if you want to excel in school you must take advantage of them while they are available. Remember you cannot know what you have not been taught. You must humble yourself and learn how to communicate with your teacher effectively for maximum result.

CHAPTER FOUR

5 SECRETS TO ANSWERING EXAM QUESTIONS

In answering exam questions, certain principles need to be considered by the students so as to enable them achieve their goals and come out with flying colors. I will quickly discuss in this chapter some proven principles that has helped millions of students around the world answer their exam questions with confidence which landed them with an excellent result to prove to others that these principles really work.

The secrets exposed here are highly recommended capsules to any student who wishes to improve his or her scores in exams without much struggle. Let's quickly have a glance at them one after the other.

1. INCREASE YOUR MOTIVATION AND CONFIDENCE

Your personal motivation and confidence is very energetic and it is responsible for increasing the level of your performance in school. This is what most people call enthusiasm it is very useful and needful to reach any height of success in life. Some students sometimes consider themselves unfit to score the highest grade in their class due to lack of self-esteem and confidence that will delete the quest for pursuit.

Your attitude towards anything is very important; you can be the best student in your class if you believe in yourself. Do not think that only a certain group of individuals in your class deserve the right to score the highest grades, or only few selected people like the class rep, class prefect, and class monitor are expected to score high in exams. Success does not respond to personalities or positions, Success only respond to anyone who is ready to apply its principles and work hard to grasp it.

You too can be the best student in your class and score high grades or even perform better than them if you believe in yourself. Be bold and willing to attempt any question and always tell yourself you can make a 100% score in that exam and you will see your result change for the better.

2. CAREFULLY STUDY THE INSTRUCTIONS AND QUESTIONS BEFORE ATTEMPTING ANSWERS

Every exam question paper is accompanied by an instruction as a guideline to that exam. Carefully read and follow the instructions cautiously before attempting the questions on the answer sheet.

Some examiners may not want you to answer all the questions but will specify the number of questions they want you to answer. Furthermore, a particular question can be made compulsory be the examiner; make sure you answer the compulsory question as it will attract more marks than the others. Do not misunderstand the questions; try to read carefully and understand the meaning of the question before attempting it because you might mistake an answer to another question if you are too excited and, in a hurry, to answer the ones you know. Avoid being confused with the words used in the context of the questions and be very careful while studying them to notice any further instructions you need to adhere to. If you perform this exercise correctly before answering your questions you will surely have an edge over your contemporaries.

3. DO NOT CRAM, GUESS OR ASSUME YOUR ANSWERS

Some students have been noted for assumption and guess work during exams and this has been discovered to be one of the major reasons why many do not attain high grades. Assumption does not guarantee success it only activates the law of probability. It is very easy for you to forget anything you cram and assumed most especially when you are running out of time in the exam hall.

Secondly, cramming will limit your understanding for a particular subject and if you are fond of cramming you will easily forget all that you have crammed the moment you finish writing that exam. Remember the exam you are writing is a test for knowledge and not test for cramming. Let your answers flow through your knowledge instead of cramming and assuming them. Avoid guess work, by guessing you are not too sure if your answer are correct or not and you will not be too sure of your scores likewise. Remember that many of the guess answers are always wrong so avoid it.

4. START WITH SIMPLE QUESTIONS

Among all the questions that are given in the question paper, you will discover that there are some of the questions that will present themselves simpler and cheaper for you to answer than others due to your studying you have little or more insight to the answers. So start answering those questions you know very well before you attempt the complex ones that you are not even very sure of the answers. Once you get the exams questions, go over them quickly and tick the ones you recognize and identify to be more familiar with and start with them immediately. Don't waste too much time trying to answer a difficult question for so long, just go straight to the ones that are easier for you to answer. You will discover that before you finish answering them more insight will come to your knowledge on how to attempt the complex ones.

5. MAKE SURE YOU UNDERSTAND THE QUESTIONS

Understanding the questions will help you to provide the correct answer that is demanded by the examiner and if you understand the questions too well your answers will be concise and straight to the point even your examiner will affirm to the fact that you know what you are doing.

6. USE YOUR TIME WISELY

Every exam has its stipulated time allocated to answer each question. If you are given one hour to complete four questions, that is fifteen minutes per question you are not expected to spend more than fifteen minutes on each question. In this case you have to be alert to meet up with the required time. Many of the questions will take less than fifteen minutes set time so apply the balance to the tougher questions. Also, do not be distracted by the ticking of the clock, just try to be fast and work with time in each question you answer. Your time is important and you should endeavor to use it judiciously so that before the overall time is elapsed you might have completed all answers waiting for submission.

Note: you are supposed to arrive at the examination venue at least 30 minutes earlier before commencement of exams to keep you in a good mood for speed. As you enter the exam hall be relaxed and say a word of prayer for a few seconds before handling your script this is to enable you command spiritual help for direction and quick remembrance of the things you have learnt.

CHAPTER FIVE

THE PREST FOMULA (Magic Capsule for Distinction)

The word PREST is gotten from the word PRESTIGE which means respect resulting from great achievement of an individual. It is therefore regarded in this lesson that if a student adopts the PREST formula adapted from the PRESTIGE word and apply it to his or academic pursuit, then he or she will definitely arrive at the end point of this formula which is A grade and automatically be rated prestigious among peers both in school and society traceable to the high performance through the adoption of the PREST formula.

Let's take a quick look at the breakdown of the PREST formula below

Mathematically, **PREST** = **A Grade**

Where	**P**	=	**PURPOSE**
	R	=	**RELATE**
	E	=	**EXAMINE**
	S	=	**STUDY**
	T	=	**TEST**

Then P + R + E + S + T = A Grade

The breakdown of the PREST formula is further explained and distributed proportionately below using building blocks for easy comprehension. Looking inside the building blocks below, you will notice that a quantity of percentage rate has been assign to each of the formula component to clearly define the relevance and the contribution of each component to the student's effort to attain a

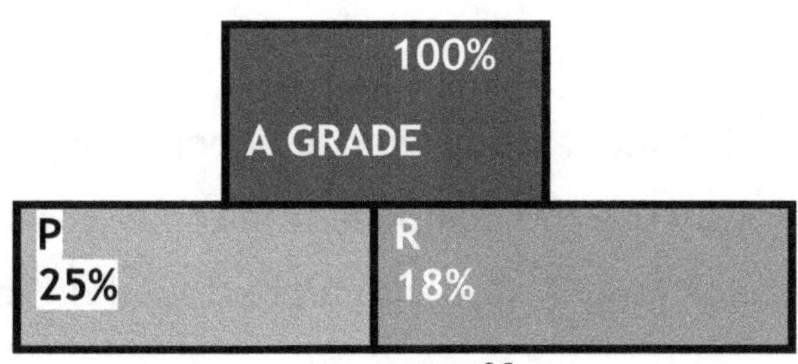

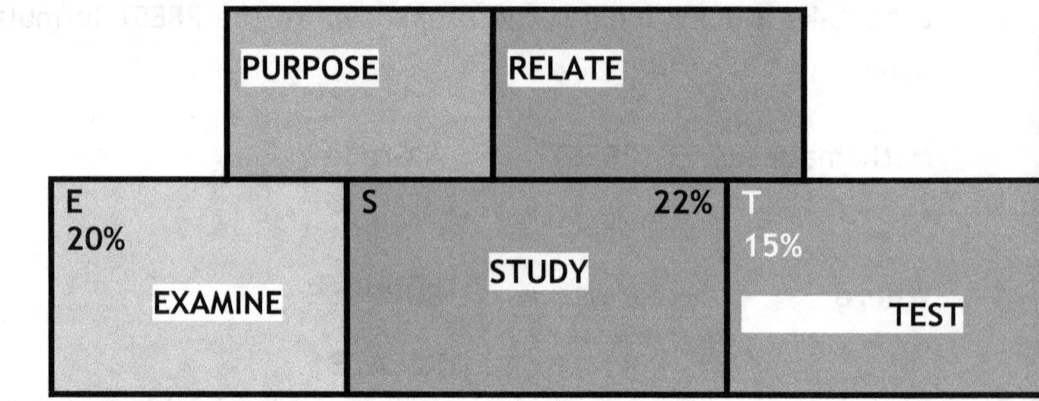

high grade in school.

Taking a careful look at the building blocks you will notice that the percentage rate allotted to each component differs according to its strength and contribution to the realization of the PREST end result in the formula which is A grade.

I.e.	P	=	25%
	R	=	18%
	E	=	20%
	S	=	22%
	T	=	15%

However, the overall student performance depends on how well the students judiciously use the component in the PREST formula to its maximum proportion. A student can be found deficient in the utilization of either one or two of the PREST formula component which will in turn affect his or her expected result. For example if a student maximizes only the P,E and S components alone, the sum of these three components will amount to 25 + 20 + 22 = 62% leaving the student at the average level. On the other hand, if a student takes advantage of the whole five component in the PREST formula, to master and maximize them all from the P - T then he or she will definitely reach the targeted dream point which is the A grade scoring 100% and then leaving the student with the excitement of an excellent student.

At this point, we will further consider the content and meaning of each component represented in the building blocks to gain proper understanding of how the PREST formula actually works like a magic for every student.

1. The **P** Block

P **25%** **PURPOSE**

The P block with its full meaning PURPOSE boldly written on it explains the role that the word purpose plays in the realization of the student dream. This component has a percentage rate of 25% which is the highest rating in the representation of other four components in the PREST formula. It clearly indicates that the quality of this component is very vital in the realization of any students dream. PURPOSE is defined as the original intent or the intention to act. This is the driving force that pulls the wheel of every action that any individual undertakes. It is very important for every student to carefully diagnose their purpose of going to school in order to give them a specified direction on where to land in their career. For me, I think that the purpose of going to school should be the very first thing every student, parent, and sponsors must first consider diligently so as to avoid failures and regrets. A strong purpose with the right mission will stir a burning desire in the student's heart to make it to the top. Secondly, if the purpose of going to school is defined by the student that singular purpose will consistently remind the student why he or she is in school at that time, or why the parents and concerned relatives decided to spend so much money to acquire education. Furthermore, your purpose as a student will continuously put a special energy and zeal to persevere in your studies despite the challenges that might surround you. I strongly recommend you to read the chapter one of this book carefully because this subject has been broadly discussed there. Just remember that if you possess a strong purpose for your academic pursuit, you are 25% ready to actualize your dream target using the PREST formula.

2. The **R** Block

R	**18%**
RELATE	

The R block also has its full meaning written boldly on it RELATE. This is the second component we will consider on the building blocks it has a percentage rate of 18% and the content of the quality in this component is very important for every student to posses but it is very surprising to note that through our research many students always neglect to take advantage of this asset, or sometimes may not even have the knowledge and awareness of this quality. The R block "RELATE" explains that a student needs to be ready to communicate and interact intelligently with other students and teachers in the school to achieve the end result of the PREST formula. As students often go to school, they meet with other peers and friends who posses either the same goal or purpose they posses, or those who posses stronger determination in achieving academic excellence. It is the duty of the student to identify and c connect with these set of students who will add value to their life to give him or her have an edge rather than stay in isolation or attach with those who will be of negative influence to them. The habit of relating and connecting with other worthy students is very important for every student to adopt because it contributes greatly to the realization of your dream. These are the few things you need to do as a student, for you to relate well with other students and teachers effectively in your school.

1. Be willing to ask questions both in class and at home
2. Be willing to join functional groups, clubs, like book review club, jet club, study group, etc.
3. Be willing to network an connect with students from other institutions that is not your own school
4. Be willing to make all your teachers become your friend.

The concept of this block id to enable the student become proactive and leverage ideas from others which will upgrade their intellectual status and develop their brains. Relating and networking with others must be tactical, try to form an alliance with people that can contribute positively to your academic pursuit not people that are eager to introduce you to corrupt ways and practice be sensitive enough to discover people with such traits and quickly do away with them before they hurt your future.

3. The **E** Block

E	**20%**
EXAMINE	

This is the third block we will consider in this chapter it has a percentage rate of 20% with its full meaning “EXAMINE” boldly written on it. Literally the word EXAMINE means look at closely or question formally. Examine is another important quality I will encourage every student to go after it with all passion. It has been proven practically by research that it is difficult for any student to forget easily what he or she took time to examine carefully. in the context of this book, and for the purpose of this chapter the word examine will mean to us the availability of the student to personal cross examination pre-examination and scrutiny in regards to the lessons he or she has received in the class. Any student that will sincerely adapt this quality and integrate it in his or her academic pursuit will be 20% ready to achieve the PREST end result. Though there are various ways a student can examine his or herself academically, but we will highlight very few of them below.

a) Set exam question from your lesson notes daily for yourself.
b) Request pre-examination from friends, classmates, relatives, parents, etc.

c) Listen to question asked by others and try to answer them yourself.
d) Avail yourself for interviews and personal assessment.

The steps of examining are also known as observing a thing and pay proper attention to it for recollection. You will notice that anything you take time to observe carefully will be retained and established within you. For instance, if your friend and family member set a pre-examination for you, and you failed some of the question after the correction take time to observe those question you failed and their answers critically you will observe that whenever you see such question again you will quickly recall the answers. Secondly the little points that were pointed out to you in class or in group discussion are always very important too to note even with those points you underline in your lesson note because they will always serve as point of reference whenever you revise them. With this kit in place in your studies, you are already 20% close to success.

4. The **S** Block

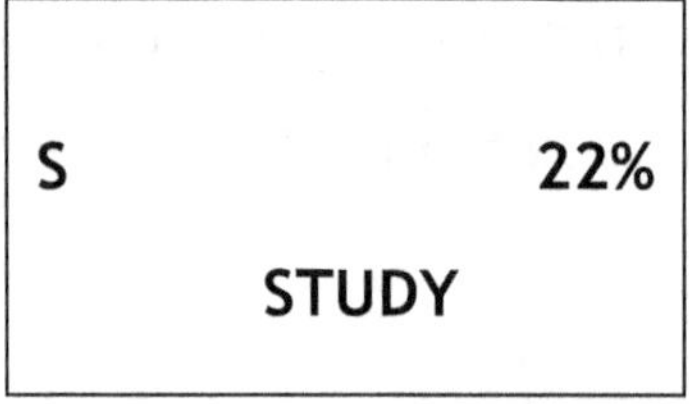

This is the fourth block of the PREST formula tool to be considered in this chapter. It is called the S block popularly known as "STUDY "with the percentage rate of 22%. The word

STUDY is the general word used by teachers, parents, relatives, friends and leaders to motivate students to work hard so as to achieve academic excellence. Although this is a proven method that has lasted the test of time and it is important for every student to utilize this tool effectively, but these groups of people listed above do not teach the students how to study in order to achieve the desired result they are only fond of using the word STUDY but do not properly educate the students how to STUDY. While there many steps to effective studying, some of which has been discussed in chapter three of this book, there are also essential steps and systems of studying I will like to point out in this book for every student to learn how to study and perform well in exams and realize the PREST formula end result through studying.

HOW TO STUDY

a) Private Study

The concept of private study is achievable when the student takes advantage of serene environments to take a close look at his or her lesson notes, text books, and other resource, materials to study them through reading. At this point the student does not need any body around him or her technology devices like phones, iPods, games, etc should be completely switched of during this pattern of studying to ensure maximum concentration and avoid unnecessary distraction.

b) Group Study

This pattern of studying is one of the oldest methods of studying that has worked for billions of people around the world and it is still working up till today if you apply it diligently to your academic life. It entails studying with like-minded people with the same goal and perceptive to achieve a desirable aim. It helps in leveraging ideas and serves as a major source of inspiration and motivation. It also helps to boost your inner strength and creativity.

c) Word Extract

This is a system of study that guarantees success at all levels. It involves a student underlining those necessary points while studying and extract them possibly into a different note book for future references and revision. This method of studying is constructive and targeted. I recommend every student to take advantage of this method and create the habit of extracting vital points, sentences, words, topics, and lessons in the course of their study.

d) Peak Hour Study

Peak period are times when circumstances and favorable conditions supports your study habit you will understand and comprehend anything you study so easily during your peak period. Your peak period can be times when you are well fed, it can be early hours of the day, afternoon or night. Studying during your peak period is the best time for students to study and be fulfilled. Discover your own peak period and make good use of it without wasting it.

5. The **T** Block

T	**15%**
TEST	

This is the fifth block on the building block that makes up the PREST formula it has it's meaning as "TEST" with the percentage rate of 15%. Without this component the actualization of the PREST end result will be incomplete, so the student needs to grip this component so dearly because this will take us to the final stage that prepares the student for any exam success. The T component TEST is categorized in various ways like pretest activities, assignments, homework, class work, home test, group test, etc. once a student test his or her ability correctly in the various modules above, then that student is said to be fit for any exam because the things the student came across during the pre test activities may repeat themselves in the final school exams. The TEST kit also takes the form of rehearsing, practicing, and mastering. The continuous practicing of a particular subject topic of a lesson received by a student will definitely build a recognition view in that student while making him or her master in that subject.

Now bringing together the five components of the PREST formula, we will have

P + R + E + S + T = PREST

25 + 18 + 20 + 22 + 15 = 100% (A grade)

Then PREST = A grade

In summary the idea behind the PREST formula is to

1. **Assist the students fulfill their academic dream of achieving A grade in exam and become the best performing student in class, school, community and nation.**

2. **Help students to be well equipped with the right information, knowledge and skills to face the demands of education in the society.**
3. **Help students fit into any level of responsibility with the excellence motivation and enthusiasm for performance.**

Students are encouraged to use this formula regularly and apply them it's components in every aspect of life and academic pursuit to produce meaningful result.

CHAPTER SIX

CHEATING SUCCESS DEADLIEST ENEMY

Most students consider cheating as their best option to pass their exams without stress to fulfill the expectation of their parents and sponsors in order to deceive them that they are performing well in school. And this set of students always depend on this malicious act to succeed and if they don't find the opportunity to cheat as planned they gradually work their way to becoming a perpetual failure. If you think it is possible to get better grades through cheating then you are wasting your time as a student. The truth is that even if you get a good grade while cheating and you were lucky enough not to be caught, you might celebrate that your score but you will not have the detailed knowledge of that subject topic, or lesson. Then sooner or later you may be required by the society to exhibit the knowledge and skills you gathered in school, either to grow a company, assist in project development, or transfer your knowledge to younger generations but then you will become a disappointment both to yourself family, community and nation.

On the other hand, if you are looking for an easy way out to pass your exams, cheating is not the best solution rather study the PREST formula in chapter five very well and make a wise decision to quit from any form of cheating you had engaged yourself in the past.

Cheating has many consequences and it is not advisable for any student with great ambition to be involved in it because it is the easiest way to destroy a student's academic career. People who engaged themselves in cheating ignorantly during their school days have not yet recovered from the bad influence and career delay this singular act has placed them. They are always regretting constantly and seeking for another opportunity to go back to school and start all over again to do it right.

The greatest enemy to exam success is cheating and the consequences of exam malpractice are so numerous that we can mention all in this book but we will look at a few very briefly.

CONSEQUENCES OF CHEATING

1. LOWERED GRADE

If you are caught in the exam hall copying someone else answers or cheating in a form of copyrighting, smuggling, body writing, phone messaging, impersonating or any other form of cheating, available your grades and score will automatically be reduced by the supervisors and invigilators, since they have been conferred with the authority to reduce your grade if caught in the exam hall cheating. Some supervisors can subtract from your score -50%, -40%, -30%, etc as the case may be. Secondly, they may decide to hand over your script to the exam malpractice committee in your school for further disciplinary action.

So instead of making additional grade to upgrade the total score, it is rather reduced to nothing left.

2. EXPULSION

Another consequence of cheating is expulsion from school which may not give the student the opportunity of attending any other school if expelled from school. When a student is caught cheating, he or she will be punished and perhaps stand the risk of being expelled from school completely.

Many students who have been found cheating have suffered this shame and mockery in their academic pursuit as some school authorities strictly adhere to this discipline that anyone caught cheating must face the examination malpractice committee and thereafter be expelled from school. Secondly the enactment of the Federal government examination malpractice decree 1999 have provide a penalty of one hundred thousand Naira fine or three years imprisonment in lieu or both such fine and imprisonment to anyone found guilty so be warned.

3. MORAL BANKRUPT

You will be morally declined and socially disconnected if you engage yourself in this act of cheating most especially if you are caught. You will always feel ashamed and guilty among your class mates and peers because they will definitely ridicule and stigmatize you as someone who cannot pass his or her own exams on merit. It will become so humiliating that each time you make a contribution or input into their discussion, they will instantly mock at you in public and point out the scene of cheating you created during exams. This scenario will always make the student loose self-respect and trust from peers and friends.

4. IGNORANCE

If you are dependent on cheating to get better grades, you will be too lazy to study or read anything that is relevant to your field of study and this will reduce your knowledge and skill in your area of study. Thereafter it will hunt you when you are required to apply the knowledge you have gained in school to improve your society, organization, office, community, and even your family.

You will also be afraid to speak to the public about your profession in the midst of other professionals and even your colleagues in school due to shortage of knowledge. However, realize that you can get better grades without cheating in any form. Getting good grades can be easy and achievable if you study and practice the PREST formula and adhere to the principles and secrets exposed in this book.

You have the potential in you to perform excellently well in school, be proud of your abilities and stop mixing up with bad friends and associates who will not help you to grow academically and fulfill your dreams.

Make a wiser decision today to work hard for your success in school and you will begin to see your grades improve for the better

Keep on succeeding.

created during exams. This scenario will always make the student loose self-respect and trust from peers and friends.

[illegible]

www.ingramcontent.com/pod-product-compliance
Lightning Source LLC
LaVergne TN
LVHW050349160826
845677LV00014B/3868

* 9 7 9 8 8 4 8 9 5 1 8 7 5 *